REKINDLING THE FLAME of CHRISTIAN EDUCATION

By

D. (JUDY) WILLIAMS

© 2004 by D. (JUDY) WILLIAMS. All rights reserved.

No part of this book may be reproduced, stored in a retrieval system, or transmitted by any means, electronic, mechanical, photocopying, recording, or otherwise, without written permission from the author.

First published by AuthorHouse 04/28/04

ISBN: 1-4184-5649-7 (e-book)
ISBN: 1-4184-4651-3 (Paperback)

Library of Congress Control Number: 2003099372

This book is printed on acid-free paper.

Printed in the United States of America
Bloomington, IN

Acknowledgements

"The Lord gave the word: great was the company of those that published it."
(Ps. 68:11)

The publication of this book must be attributed to all my friends, family and spiritual associates.
I would like to acknowledge and express heartfelt thanks to the following:

- I shall be eternally grateful to my family members; my husband Anthony and my sons Lehron, Lorin and Joshua for their patience and moral support while I laboured relentlessly at nights to complete this book.

- To my parents, Mr. & Mrs. Ashton Gould for your profound spiritual impact on my life and for your continued support in ministry.

- Dr. Cecil Johnson, Ph.D., of Christian Bible College for his careful review of my Thesis on Education and hence his valid suggestion for publication of the same.

- Pastor Al Ebanks of Agape Family Worship Centre (my Pastor) who tediously examined the manuscript for biblical and theological accuracy. Thank you Pastor Al for all your helpful comments and profound biblical insight.

- Mr. George Boldeau, who took time out of his very busy schedule to edit the manuscript in its initial draft form.

- Jasmine Powell who faithfully rendered literary guidance

- Pearline Donalds, my friend and Ministry Partner who shared my vision on this subject and with encouraging words and needed support, stuck with me until the manuscript was completed.

Dedication

In memory of my beloved father
Ashton Gould
July 1917 – February 2004

Table of Contents

Acknowledgements iii
Dedication v
Foreword ix
Introduction xi
Methodology and Purpose xiii
Synopsis xv
Chapter One 1
History of Christian Education 1
   1.1 Christian Education – What it is? 1
   1.2 Historical Perspective of the Christian Education 3
   1.3 Old Testament Pedagogy 4
   1.4 New Testament Principles and Practices 7
   1.5 Christian Education After the Apostles 10
   1.6 The Middle Ages 11
   1.7 The Renaissance 13
   1.8 The Reformation, Christian Education & Martin Luther 15
   1.9 The Progression of Christian Education & Other Developments 20
Chapter Two 24
The Decline of Christian Education 24
   2.1 Circumstances, People & Events Influencing Traditional Christian Education 24

    2.2   The Enlightenment 29

    2.3   Secular Humanism & the Curriculum (in the U.S.A.) 32

    2:4   The New Age Movement and the World Core Curriculum. 35

    2.6   Observations 39

Chapter Three 41

Rekindling the Flame of Christian Education 41

    3.1   Rekindle the Flame! 41

    3.2   Secular School vs. Christian School 42

    3.3   Why Christian Education? 46

    3.4   A Christian Based Curriculum 47

    3.5   The Role of a Teacher of Christian Education 52

    3.6   Teaching Methods for the Christian School 56

    3.7   Lessons from the Master Teacher 57

    3.8   Recommendations to Rekindle the Flame of Christian Education 59

    3.9   Conclusion 62

Bibliography 65

Endnotes 69

Foreword

Those with zeal to teach must strategically place themselves in the position of a learner". Delfene (Judy) Williams in rekindling the flame of christian education give a well researched and thought provoking look in the historical development of education from a biblical viewpoint. This book will be a valuable resource to any serious learner, interested in the subject of education from a distinct Christian perspective. It identifies key movers and shakers in the development of Christian education, speaks to current problems and their roots and offers practical suggestions on how we can rekindle the flame of christian education in our generation.

Proverbs 9:9 says "Give instruction to a wise man, and he will be still wiser, teach a just man and he will increase in learning".

Pastor Al Ebanks
Agape Family Worship Centre, Cayman Islands

Introduction

This paper serves to demonstrate that current trends in Christian education represent a significant decline from the high standards associated with the theological fundamental perspectives of the past.

In examining the history of education, one will discover that its foundational, principles and practices are clearly laid out in the Old Testament. The contents of the Torah provided the essential norms for a productive life that stressed the nature and character of God and what his requirements are for all humanity. Others were in the form of traditions and customs handed down from generation to generation.

The biblical standard of education originated with God when he instructed Adam in the Garden of Eden. Moses, an Old Testament patriarch became one of the earliest contributors to biblical education. Through direct communication, Moses received instructions from Almighty God who assigned him the responsibility to teach his Laws to the Hebrew people. Subsequently, Christ was the greatest of all teachers. He spent most of his time teaching his disciples, preparing them to be teachers among all people. Jesus placed so much emphasis on the area of teaching and later commissioned his followers to *"go and teach all nations"*.

Christian education was never without serious challenges. During the 2nd century, a dangerous heresy in the form of Gnosticism entered the church and spread rapidly. This distorted Old Testament scriptures by attacking the basic principles of Christianity and criticizing its underlying philosophy and education. Throughout the ages, movements such as this have had a disturbing negative impact on the quality of Christian education. The greatest damage was done by the destructive influence of Secular Humanist during the second half of the 20th century.

This study aims to review the developments of Christian education by carefully examining the work of various educators and historical movements that have affected these developments. Also in light of current Christian educational trends, this study will outline developmental strategies and innovative approaches to rekindle the flame of Christian Education.

It is my prayer that fellow Christian educators reading this paper will be challenged to deliver a high standard of Christian Education that is relevant to the times in which we live, in order to bring believers to maturity in Christ and enhance the quality of the Christian life.

Methodology and Purpose

This study draws upon a variety of articles, reports as well as research and observations of individuals/educators in order to examine the development of education, its fundamental principles and practices as it relates to the Christian faith. The main purpose is to evaluate current trends in Christian education in relation to past biblical standards that were of worthwhile significance and to determine that there has been a decline from previous standards. The following areas will be explored:

a) Christian education of past significance including Old and New Testament practices.
b) Events, factors or ideals affecting Christian education.
c) Contributors to the progress of Christian education

It is the intention of the writer to approach the subject by way of careful analysis so as to expose problems in current developments and recommend positive solutions.

Included in this paper are developmental approaches and practical solutions that can bring about much needed reform in order to educate our children effectively in this 21st century. This study is important for the following reasons:

a) to highlight present problems in current secular curriculum
b) to identify appropriate strategies that will bring about change in current trends, and
c) to offer practical solutions in rekindling the flame of Christian education.

Wherever possible, a chronological sequence of approach will be maintained in this analysis, however, one will find that dates may sometimes overlap. Finally, the paper is written using UK English, hence spelling of some words will differ from that of American English.

Synopsis

Chapter 1 – *The History of Christian Education*

This chapter seeks to define the subject of this study and continues with a brief history of Christian Schools from the ancient past, highlighting methodological and pedagogical implications of Old Testament Jewish times, and the New Testament procedures.. Historical developments in the periods known as the Middle Ages, the Renaissance, the Reformation and the Enlightenment will also be explored.

Chapter 2 – *The Decline of Christian Education*

In this chapter we examine the progression of post reformation Christian education in light of prevailing factors, events, circumstances or Individuals which affected educational trends. It specifically describes how the Enlightenment and Secular Humanism have had a negative impact on the curriculum to the extent of promoting secular education at the expense of Christian education. It also includes observations relating to the decline of Christian education and the rise of secular education.

Chapter 3 – *Rekindling the flame of Christian education*

This chapter discusses the necessity for a return to the fundamental principles of a Biblical standard of education, the role of the teacher, the curriculum and the exemplary teaching methods that Jesus used. The paper recommends the promotion of Christian education by suggesting that a special week be designated "Christian Education Awareness Week" when a series of events highlights various aspects of a sound Christian education system.

Chapter One

History of Christian Education

1.1 Christian Education – What it is?

It is imperative that the term Christian education be understood in order to determine its outcome and what is really expected. The following definitions were cited.

a) *"It is the harmonious development of the physical, the mental and spiritual powers. It prepares the student for the joy of service in this world and for the higher joy of wider service in the world to come."*[1]

b) Pazmino, quoted the following definitions from Werner C. Graendorf and Lawrence A. Cremin: *"Christian education is a Bible-based, Holy Spirit-empowered (Christ-centered) teaching-learning process. It seeks to guide individuals at all levels of growth through contemporary teaching means toward knowing and experiencing God's purpose and plan through Christ in every aspect of living. It also equips*

> them for effective ministry, with the overall focus on Christ the Master Educator's example and his command to make mature disciples."[2]

c) *"Christian education is the deliberate, systematic, and sustained divine and human effort to share or appropriate the knowledge, values, attitudes, skills, sensitivities, and behaviors that comprise or are consistent with the Christian faith. It fosters change, renewal, and reformation of persons, groups and structures by the power of the Holy Spirit to conform to the revealed will of God as expressed in the Scriptures and preeminently in the person of Jesus Christ, as well as any outcomes of that effort"*.[3]

From the definitions given above, the mission and purpose of the educational process can clearly be formulated. God, and his purposes, is the subject to be imparted by the educator and the intended outcome is the transformation of the learner by the power of the Holy Spirit to <u>becoming</u> God's representative in all areas of life. Christian education means more than just pursuing a course of study for personal accomplishment, but as we see in E. G. White's definition above, *"It is the harmonious development of the entire human dimensions, mental, physical, spiritual, and social"*. Therefore Christian education will prepare individuals to live godly and productive lives now and in preparation for the life to come. On the other hand, Christian education does not ignore the value of knowledge of non religious studies such as the arts and languages. The morals and values imparted into the minds of the learners will give them a more positive perspective of life equipping them with requisite skills, so that they will not succumb to the evils of the world such as violence, lawlessness, drugs, careless life styles and illicit sexual activities. Instead, they will be committed to wholesome family relationships, church life and service to the community.

1.2 Historical Perspective of the Christian Education

It is impossible to consider Christian education without reviewing the significant contributions of educators and the pedagogical imperatives found in historical data. By studying the methods and techniques of earlier contributors to education as well as events and other factors that affected educational trends, the Christian educator will be able to identify principles, strategies and goals that have been applicable and may be of lasting value to education. Thus the past serves as an ever-present tutor for present and future educational guidelines. Accordingly, former methodologies and educational strategies that were effective in the past may be adapted into modern approaches to teaching and learning. As we consult the past, it is necessary to find out what factors contributed to the educational development and growth in godliness and how educational efforts fostered this development. We need to find out how these biblical principles were conveyed in order to educate effectively for this living faith. We should consider if the needs of persons were addressed efficiently, what biblical demands were formulated in this response, and how the biblical demands were interpreted and applied in those particular settings. It is also important to identify what vision, concept and rationale "grounded" effective educational work and how these were communicated. Essentially, if mistakes made by past educators are ignored then there is the possibility of repeating them. However, by identifying the mistakes of the past, valuable lessons can be learnt, and we could initiate appropriate solutions rather than create further problems.

In reviewing the historical information on the subject of education, one can easily appreciate the fact that God's divine intervention was obviously, working through creation and the lives of various individuals to bring about a biblical system of education. We can also observe how God revealed and transmit his truth; building upon Judaism, the revelation of Jesus Christ. The rapid spread of the Christianity after Pentecost, significantly influenced education, the roots of which was deeply embedded in the Hebrew Scriptures. Therefore the value and timelessness of these principles are relevant and applicable for today's education and should not be ignored.

History shows that the church had developed various agencies and instruments to fulfill its educational task. This was mainly for initiating converts both old and young alike into the faith, and influencing the practices and beliefs of the Christian community. Therefore the Christian church provided the context in which to consider the heritage of Christian education. This study commence by reviewing the pre-Christian sources of the Old Testament times and proceeds through the ages to the present.

1.3 Old Testament Pedagogy

From the early pages of scripture one can see the institution of the first school established right there in the Garden of Eden by God, with himself as instructor, nature as the curriculum and Adam and Eve as students. So important was education to God that often he would enter the Eden classroom in the cool of the day to instruct his students. He could have sent an angel, but instead he chose to go in person. He instructed Adam and Eve in relation to looking after the Eden classroom, *"to dress it and to keep it"* Gen 2:15, among others things. A major assignment was for Adam to name all of the animals in the garden.

Moses was rooted and grounded in the doctrines and principles of Jewish theology by his mother during the early years of his life when she nursed him as the son of Pharaoh's daughter. He was later educated in Egyptian schools. However, it was the early training of his mother that had molded and influenced his life and prepared him for the greater task as God's representative. Moses later emerged as leader of the children of Israel which include the responsibility to teach them.

Through the teachings of Moses, the believing community was required to relate their faith in God to all of life's situations. In Deut 6:4-9 we see the educational mandate which required passing down the commandments to the next generation. Basically, the ultimate goal for this was to foster a love for God to be expressed in loyalty and obedience to his commandments. This passage also gives valuable insight about the teacher, the goals, the students, the content of the curriculum and the setting of biblical education.

It is important to note that such settings included the various opportunities of parents to impress Godly values upon the hearts of their children. These are recorded as times *'when sitting at home, when walking along the road, when lying down,* etc'. Symbolic reminders of the commandments were placed upon the *foreheads, doorposts, gates and houses.* The book of Proverbs also admonishes that children be attentive to the instructions of their parents. From this we see God, as the instigator of biblical education, the author and discloser of the Christian faith. Throughout the book of Deuteronomy, many essential insights are given for understanding the nature and history of education. The educational principles of Deut 30:11-20; 31:9-13; and 31:30-3:4 were demonstrated in Jesus' life and ministry. Therefore, the Christian educator is challenged to:

a) Make clear God's offer of life and death and encourage the choosing of the spiritual life to be found in Jesus Christ.

b) Emphasize the importance of reading and hearing God's law, which was an heritage to be shared with all in the community of faith.

c) Foster the liberation of persons and facilitate worship. This demonstrates an education that stimulates growth in the Christian faith, liberation, and causes one to become spiritually refreshed. Individuals are able to become all that God intended them to be in worship and celebration while attributing worth to God.

The method of teaching prescribed by God and conveyed in his instructions to Moses at that time, was intended for the nation of Israel. Teaching included instructions and admonition. They were instructed on God's truth and demands while the admonition was to challenge persons in their way of life. Education was centred on the Torah – the Law of God which was first communicated orally then written in the scriptures to convey the moral and spiritual revelation of God. It also reveals that God's primary objective was for the education of their children. Education began at an early age – from first consciousness. The purpose of biblical education in Old Testament times was to develop an awareness of God which further resulted in transformed lives.

Education placed great emphasis on the family, a system that had prevailed during the days of the patriarchs while God provided the conditions most favourable for the development of character. The home was the setting of Jewish education and the responsibility of teaching was firmly placed on the parents. Jewish education was entirely religious and the Jewish textbook was the Holy Scriptures. Primary education was to prepare the child to read the law while higher education concerned the actual reading and memorizing of the law. Detailed knowledge of the law was pertinent to the higher aim of education, which required the training of disciples in the knowledge of God. "Synagogues and schools were established during and prior to the exile where the Hebrew language, oral traditions and written scriptures was being taught."[4]

Methodology used in teaching was oral communication along with memory aids such as poetry, word play and acrostic. Visual aids were also used in teaching (Exodus 12:1-28; Deut 6:4-9; Josh 4:1-24) along with music and Psalms. Teaching was conducted at scheduled times and on various spontaneous occasions such as during the celebration of feast days. The feasts themselves served to impart education on the history of the nation. Again the sole purpose of these teaching efforts was that the individual learners would bring honour and credit to the name of God and their families throughout their lives.

"The two events that ushered in the beginning of public schools are the publication of Deuteronomy in 621 BC and the work of Ezra"[5]. Under the leadership of Ezra, the Torah, in its written form was accepted as the regulating norm in every aspects of Jewish life. The Torah required interpretation and explanation and also needed to be expounded and this took place in the synagogue. The growth of these small learning institutions continued as a result of the conditions of exile. Hence, the synagogue became the centre of public Jewish education and was sometimes referred to as the "religious university".

It was in the synagogue that Jewish elementary schools evolved. Although reading, writing and arithmetic were taught, the primary objective was the teaching of the Hebrew Scriptures. They were expected first to learn the alphabets then to memorize the Pentateuch. The scribes were well-learned men who had the responsibility to teach and regarded this task as holy.

1.4 New Testament Principles and Practices

Observations during the New Testament period reveal that the early education of Jesus' disciples followed the Jewish pattern of worship and learning. Several New Testament books reflected the Jewish method of education. For example, some learned in family settings. Timothy was influenced by his grandmother Lois and mother Eunice, II Tim 1:5; 3:15. The Ethiopian Eunuch was instructed by Philip, prior to coming to the faith, Acts 8:36-40. Paul was thoroughly trained in the Law under the tutelage of Gamaliel in Jerusalem, Acts 5:34; 22:3. Paul utilized this training to become an effective advocate of the faith among the Gentiles and Jews. "Education gradually became a distinctive way of life for God's chosen people. Christians were identified as followers of the way (Acts 9:2; 24:14)"[6].

Similar to Old Testament practices, the disciples of Jesus were commissioned to teach others to obey all that Jesus had commanded them. Instructions considered as required information for 'new' converts is found in the following text: 1 Cor 15:3-8; Phil 2:5-11; 1 Tim 3:16; 2 Tim 2:11-13 and Titus 3:4-7. In time, official teachers arose after the rabbinic pattern whose responsibilities included the preservation, transmission and interpretation of essential truths to the Christian community.

It is impossible to focus on the history of Christian education without highlighting the significant contribution made by Jesus and the fundamental aspects of his work. It was said of him in the scriptures, *"He taught as one having authority"*. Jesus seized every opportunity to teach, for example, the woman caught in adultery and the storm on the lake. He started where the learners were at, using objects, word pictures and story subjects with which the learners were familiar, e.g. boats, fish, sheep, water, wine, bread, fig trees, seeds, grains, etc. Jesus knew that effective learning build upon the previous knowledge of the learner. He challenged his learners to discover truth, by asking questions that provoked their thinking, thereby motivating them to provide the answers. Jesus also gave the learner the opportunity to practice what they learned as in the case of the rich young ruler. He instructed, and then challenged him to sell all his possessions.

Herman Horne gives us a wonderful illustration of Jesus' pedagogical approach in the following:[7] In John chapter 4:1-42 is an example of Jesus seizing a teachable moment. First we need to take into consideration the circumstances that are conducive to the teaching and learning experience. These are the teacher, the student, the environment, the curriculum, the aims, the teaching method and the objective – intended outcome for the learner.

In analyzing the text we see from the following that all was in place for a teaching situation:

1) The teacher – Jesus

2) The student – the woman of Samaria

3) The environment – Jacob's well in Samaria

4) The Curriculum – the water of life

5) Aims – transforming a life

6) Method – Conventional; Jesus initiated conversation based on her personal needs. This stimulated her interest and encouraged her to communicate. He in turn builds on her replies. Notice his contrast between the water from Jacob's well and the water of life. Also note his use of motivation to stimulate interest.

In this instance, Jesus found himself with the ideal setting for a teaching situation and made use of the opportunity. At other times we see Jesus using word pictures in his communication, through parables to illustrate various key points.

He later commissioned his disciples to *"go and teach all nations"* Matt 28:19, a mission which they took seriously, spreading the Christian faith and the pattern of Christian education to the ends of the earth.

As the spread of Christianity continued, various educational efforts were implemented to deal with the challenges of interpreting the faith. These included periods of training prior to acceptance into the faith. The curriculum for Christian education included reinterpretation or interpretation of the Old Testament Scriptures. This was due largely to the fact that many converts were not Jews so their first exposure to Old Testament Scriptures needed interpretation. They found it difficult to understand how Jesus' life and ministry related to God's previous dealings with his people. Also interpretation was needed in light of Jesus' claim as the Messiah.

Included in the curriculum was the confession of faith. This was an affirmation of Jesus' Lordship elaborated upon in the Apostles creed and teachings of "the Way". These were moral expectations of followers of Christ also known as "followers of the Way", outlined in the Didache.

The early church was at risk of becoming annihilated hence the emphasis was placed on order and discipline using clear guidelines to carry out training instructions.

Teaching continued even after the death of the Apostles. "As early as AD 80-110, the Didache emerged as an essential instructional manual, primarily for new converts to Christianity"[8]. Ignatius, a Bishop from Antioch urged that children be taught the Holy Scriptures and a skilled trade. The aspect of learning a trade originated with the Jews in Old Testament times when they taught their sons a skill along with biblical and literary learning.

As a result of Jesus' commission to teach, newcomers to the faith were taught in their homes. This was known as "catecheumins" which indicates that they were taught orally, utilizing the method of questions & answers. This was required for baptism and church membership. Male and female had to undergo a 2-3 year period of instruction as preparation for baptism and church membership.

> *Formal catechetical schools with strong literary emphasis were established as a result of the catechetical instructions. These schools provided the theological foundations for future Christian leaders such as **Origen** (185 – 254) known as the prince of Christian learning and **Athanasius** (ca 296 – 378).[9] " Although Christian doctrine was the primary focus of education, some schools like the one at Alexandria included mathematics and medicine in their curriculum. Still later, grammar was added by Origen who was the most famous Alexandrian writer. He led the school from 202 – 232 then moved to Caesarea Palestine where he continued his teaching career for another twenty years. He is often called the first great theologian and brought to scientific formulation the allegorical interpretation of scripture. His writings numbered in thousands and include commentaries on the Bible. "The catechetical schools exerted a strong influence in Christian circles and also in Roman society at large. Their existence says William Boyd, had far reaching effects. Through them, "Christianity became for the first time a definite factor in the culture of the world.[10]*

1.5 *Christian Education After the Apostles*

Teaching was the motivation of all those who became part of the Christian faith. In II Tim 3:2, Paul indicated that one of the qualifications of a bishop was the ability to teach. He also made reference to various instances of teaching taking place in Ephesus, Corinth, Rome and Thessalonica. Jews, primarily valued formal education but Jesus' disciples had more compelling reason to stress the importance of teaching based on the mandate given them by him. After the death of the Apostles, teaching continued and the Didache was adopted as the instructional manual for new converts to the

Christian faith. Around A.D. 150, **Justin Martyr**, a great scholar of the Christian church, established church schools in Ephesus, Rome, Alexandria and Egypt. **Clement** (150 – 21) established schools with a wonderful reputation and maintained this excellent reputation, as a great pioneer of the Christian schools for more than a century.

Catechetical schools provided theological and literary foundations for future Christian leaders. Scholars such as Origen (185 – 254) (dubbed the Prince of Christian learning) was educated at catechetical schools. These schools had a major impact and influence in Christian circles and at that time Roman society at large. Through these Catechetical schools, Christianity began to have a definite influence on the culture of the world.

1.6 The Middle Ages

The middle ages witnessed a change in the role of the biblical standard of education due to the spread of Christianity and the advancement of the Christian faith. Also the fall of Rome gave rise to the church as a social institution with continuing influence that had a profound impact upon education.

AD 500-1000 – Formal education was conducted in monastic and cathedral schools as well as universities. After AD 800 their curricula emphasized the 7 liberal arts. Some of these schools later grew into universities where the study of law and other subjects were undertaken to prepare students for professional careers outside the church. As the universities sought to produce scholastic minded professionals, the family declined from its important role in educating for the faith. This resulted in a rise in alternative institutions. Western societies and education were heavily shaped by Christianity, mainly by the Roman Catholic Church which operated monastery schools at elementary levels. Merchant and craft guilds also maintained some schools that provided a basic education and training in specific crafts.

It was during the 11th century that medieval scholars developed "**Scholasticism**, a philosophical and educational movement that used both human reasoning and revelations for the interpretation of the

Bible. They had discovered the work of Aristotle and other Greek philosophers resulting in an attempt to reconcile Christian theology with Greek philosophy. This influenced the theology and philosophy of Christian Europe during the second half of the middle ages. Scholasticism comes from the Latin word *scholasticus* pertaining to a school – medieval church school. This new ideology destroyed faith in God and the Bible and was a direct revolt against traditional theology and biblical philosophy, meanwhile promoting interest in the individual and his freedom. Universities such as Paris, Oxford and Cambridge came about as a result of the Scholastics-led intellectual revival of the 12th and 13th century." (New Standard Encyclopedia)

"Meanwhile those who continued to practice the Christian faith had taken on worship as a new method of teaching.

> *Worship unto the Almighty became one of the primary vehicles of education by teaching lessons of faith to the participants through its richness. Worship included daily mass, religious drama and various other Christian festivals associated with the liturgical calendar and celebrated throughout the year. This was the way the Christian message was conveyed to a largely illiterate population of people who had no other access to formal Christian education.*[11] "

Israel Galindo states,

> *Worship, as an authentic Christian teaching approach has a long history in the life of the church. The unique nature of Christian teaching requires attention to the whole person: spirit, soul and body.*
>
> *In terms of teaching for an effectual faith, the corporate worship experience addresses all of the pertinent personal components: cognitive, affective, behavioral, and volitional as noted below:*"[12]

The cognitive relates to ideas, knowledge, understanding and comprehension. Worship experience connected to the cognitive includes, preaching, readings, prayers hymn text and the intentional proclamation of our corporate identity.

The affective domain deals with feelings and emotions. Components of worship affecting these areas include music, memories, fellowship, spiritual manifestations, ambiance, feelings and moods, drama, dance affection towards God and people, love for God and people, etc.

The behavioral domain is expressed in action and conduct also in thinking. Areas of the worship experience that are behavioral are expressions of praise and worship including movements, participation, prayers and responses

The volitional relates to passion, will and conviction. Worship is an expression of belief but certain circumstances require more than belief. It requires an act of faith especially in times of doubt and pain.

From the four components we understand that worship was a contributing factor to Christian education. We also learn from the scriptures that activities at religious gatherings included singing of the Psalms, readings from the Holy Scriptures, praying and other expressions of worship.

1.7 The Renaissance

The Renaissance was a period in history known as the revival, reawakening, or rebirth of learning and culture. This took place over the approximate period of (1400-1600) and also marks the transition from the middle-ages to the modern. The Renaissance opened up new aspects of life in the area of education. Literature, art, science and religion were coming to the forefront while the physical world was expanding through amazing geographical discoveries resulting in what is considered the "new world". Coinciding with this event was a rise in **humanist** ideologies, where at this focal point in human history, the emphasis was placed on human beings rather than on God and eternity. This phase of the renaissance fostered humanities in education, studies that are designed primarily to promote culture on the one hand and on the other, to help students make a living. It is in direct contrast to the practical studies which prepared the entire individual for the working world which came about as a result of scholars revolting against the traditional interest in religion.

During the period of the Renaissance, Christian education was profoundly affected and other areas of studies took on precedence. Education grew to be of great importance to individual States where emphasis was placed on education for service to society and the state, and political tension developed between the papacy and the princes and rulers of these states. The invention of the printing press in the mid-15th century and other technological developments made self-education possible. The printing of religious books stimulated interest in religion. Moslem and Jewish scholarships gave way to curricular expansion along with studies in additional areas such as humanities. Humanities include languages such as the study of ancient Greek and Latin classics, literature and philosophy, as well as history, mathematics and the arts.arts and sciences.

This period of intellectual, artistic awakening and rebirth spread from Italy, France, Germany England and Spain into the other countries of Europe. In France the movement bore a rich harvest in literature, a school of painting was established in the Netherlands and Flanders, while in Germany humanistic philosophy was the strongest expression.

The Renaissance also caused the theory on reason and logics of the Greek philosopher Socrates to resurface. *"Socrates stressed the place of reason and logic, with thinking itself viewed as objective reasoning. He said human reason was the means by which to discern divine revelation and its implications for all of life. He also stressed the importance of life but not in terms of the God of the Hebrews."*[13] This presents questions such as the place of human reason in relation to the Christian faith. There is also the question of doubt and reasoning. These questions created opportunities for personal discovery using the capacities of human reason created by God. Christian education therefore had to address areas of moral, ethical and character formation to supplement intellectual training but not in a way that violated the worth and dignity of persons as God's creatures.

Prior to the reformation, Wycliffe's disciples and the Hussites (1369-1415) had printed the Scriptures in the vernacular. They also developed a system of schools and a university to promote practical Christianity.

The renaissance focused on people, primarily the elite, and on cultural and intellectual renewal. Traditional knowledge itself was the goal irrespective of God or revelation. New interest in science also created a shift in the curricula of schools. This was due to the scientific revolution which stemmed from enquiries of Roger Bacon. So the renaissance witnessed the humanization of knowledge and the beginning of the reformation movement in the established church.

1.8 The Reformation, Christian Education & Martin Luther

The Renaissance had awakened a new zeal for reformation in matters of religious significance, namely the ecclesiastical functions of the church. There were many practices in the Catholic Church which violated the Christian faith, some of which included the sale of indulgences in exchange for eternal life and the severe persecutions that were mercilessly inflicted on the peasants. Many attempts were made to bring about religious reformation but the Catholic Church showed great resistance to change.

Martin Luther (1483 – 1546)

Many of the better educated people came to recognize the fallacy of the Catholic Church in its doctrine and practices. The church had strayed from the principles of the Holy Scriptures. Martin Luther, an Augustinian monk, emerged as a great advocate of reformation and education in 1517. He publicly denounced the practices of the Catholic Church and bravely defended his position using the Holy Scriptures as grounds for his arguments in the 95 theses which he

REKINDLING THE FLAME of CHRISTIAN EDUCATION

nailed on the door of the church at Wittenberg. *"The general principles of the reformation were:*

    a)   The Holy Scriptures as sole authority for faith and life.

    b)   Justification by faith alone without the merits of good works

    c)   The priesthood of all believers

    d)   The Bible must be interpreted with the aid of the Holy Spirit."[14]

The authority of the Bible was emphasized while there was a call to return to the Christian faith. "These principles of reformation fostered a new vision for Christian education universally. This was to train Christians to become priests of the living God."[15]

Luther recognized that there was a link between reform both in the school and in the church. He realized that how you live on earth is of importance for eternal life. He saw the task of Christian education as sound biblical instructions that equipped the individual for service to God in this life and prepared them for life in the heavenly realm. His three arguments supporting the necessity of Christian education was "1) *to protect the children from the Devil's attempt to keep them away from God, 2) If God allowed education to take place we should not reject it, 3) it is a command of God in Ps. 78: 5-6."*[16]

> *Luther was original in building a curriculum from the Bible. He said Biblical instructions are what makes the school a Christian school and that the Holy Scriptures must be a subject in itself and must permeate all other subjects."* Together with Melanchthon, Luther devised *a school order which helped to bring about the first public school. It was Luther who originally placed emphasis on parental obligation in education and emphasized the need for curriculum and textbooks.* "*Luther's goal for Christian education was to "fight the Devil" and according to 2 Tim 3:15 "to know the*

> *Bible". Children were taught to bring honour and glory to God through biblical instructions.*[17]

Although Luther's educational philosophies focused on the home and government, he was one of the first to emphasize the need for compulsory education. His motivation was that all persons should be able to read the Bible. Additionally, he urged the study of languages, grammar, rhetoric logic, literature, poetry, history, music, mathematics, gymnastics and nature study.

For Luther, catechism was second to the scripture in order of importance. It was an important item in the curriculum as it explained the Ten Commandments, the Lord's prayer, the Apostles Creed and basic theological concepts.

Luther viewed music as important, and believes a schoolmaster must be able to sing. History tells us that Luther played several instruments and had a good voice.

As mentioned earlier, Luther made significant contributions to Christian education and he considered *"discipline as an important ingredient of the teaching methodology. He was a strong believer in obedience on the part of both children at home and students in the classroom."*[18]

His teaching methods include imagery, illustrations and repetition. He objected to information overload. His positive imprint on the history of Christian education is unmistakable and one will agree that the former monk became one of the greatest preachers and teachers of all time. As a result of Luther's protest against the doctrines and practices of the Catholic Church, Protestantism became a major division of Christianity.

Both the renaissance and the reformation expanded the curriculum beyond the traditional areas of study. While the renaissance was an expression of culture and intellect, the reformation was theological and ecclesiastical. Religious reformers extended literacy to the masses by establishing vernacular primary schools that offered reading, writing, arithmetic and religion for children in their own language.

Life and education was centred upon God, while humans were considered to be God's creation with definite responsibilities and privileges. The reformation catered to ALL people of all classes. Spiritual renewal was primary because human reason was viewed as fallen and subject to God's revelation in scripture. Reformers relied upon the Bible.

Developmental aspects of Christian Education

Erasmus (1466 – 1536) - Like Luther, Erasmus was influential in the development of Christian education during the reformation. He was dubbed 'prince of the humanists' or 'the most famous of all humanists. Robert Ulich, writing about Erasmus said *"few men have molded European education as decisively as Erasmus. He encouraged a better method of teaching and a more understanding and tolerant attitude toward the pupil and he infiltrated classical studies with a spirit of exactness, historical criticism and international perspective. This allowed ancient philosophy to dominate the humanities until the beginning of the 19th century."*[19]

Erasmus, a humanist Roman Catholic, was literary rather than evangelical stirring people to think rather than act as Luther did. He viewed education as necessary and believes that man without education has no humanity at all. He believed that teachers were of more importance than the school system. He recognized Jesus as the perfect example of a model teacher and patterned all learning objectives on him.

> *He insisted on a core curriculum that would develop intellect as the center of man – the classics, the writings of the church fathers and the Bible. His finest work 'Liberal Education of Boys' was published 1529.*
>
> *He criticized the church openly and especially it's Bible – the Latin Vulgate. This he considered untrustworthy, full of errors and a rather inadequate translation. He was nonetheless considered a great contributor to education.*[20]

1.9 The Progression of Christian Education & Other Developments

Co-Education

It appears that Christians were the first to teach both genders in school-like settings, e.g. the Catechetical classes. Both male and female were required to learn the rudiments of the Christian faith and were thus taught prior to acceptance into the community of believers. W.M. Ramsey states,

> *Christianity's aim was universal education, not education confined to the rich, as among the Greeks and Romans...and it (made) no distinction of sex. Many historians indicated that the formal education of the Romans prior to Christ, was in the literary skills and was limited to boys which were from the privileged class.*[21]

The principle of teaching both sexes was demonstrated by Jesus in his teaching which the church has never neglected. So we see that as a result of the church not adopting the Greco-Roman practices of excluding girls, coeducation was widely accepted and practiced at all levels of Western societies, and later other regions of the world.

Universal Education

Christianity was available to all mankind, regardless of gender, class or nationality. Therefore individuals from all social status or ethnic background were taught especially in preparation for church membership. By the time of Luther, this practice had deteriorated and ignorance was widespread. As a result of this, in 1529 Luther wrote his *small catechism*. In this he noted that the common people had little or no knowledge of Christian teachings and the pastors were incompetent to teach. Cultivating the mind was essential for Luther so *"he urged a state school system to include vernacular primary schools for both sexes as well as Latin secondary schools and universities."*[22]

> ***John Calvin**, another leader in the Protestant Reformation, also supported universal education. Calvin's system of elementary education included reading, writing, arithmetic, grammar and religion. His plan included the establishment of secondary schools for the purpose of training citizens for civil and ecclesiastical leadership.*[23]

The desire of both Luther and Calvin to educate universally shows that universal education has its origin in Christianity, based on biblical tenets that God is no respecter of persons (Acts 10:34). Since each individual is personally responsible for his/her own salvation, everyone needs to be educated.

Compulsory education

Among Luther's contribution to Christian education was the value he places upon education for all. He told civic authorities that they should compel children to attend school. Although his idea of compulsory education was rather slow in taking off, it soon spread to other parts of Europe. It reached France a hundred years later when a Roman Catholic priest advocated it. Compulsory school education was taken on by Western societies and has extended across the world to the extent of being enshrined in Law. Today compulsory school education is an acceptable norm thanks to the great Reformer, Martin Luther.

Graded Education

Lutheran layman, **John Sturm** (1507–1589) introduced the system of graded education with the hope that students would be motivated to study. The incentive was that they should be able to advance to a higher level.

Kindergarten

Friedrich Froebel (1782-1852) was the mastermind behind the concept of Kindergarten. He was the son of a Lutheran pastor and a devout Christian. This stemmed from an idea he had while assisting his father in the family garden. He envisioned a garden where young children could come and grow under the care of an expert gardener – a teacher who would cultivate minds. In 1855 the first Kindergarten school in the USA was started by Mrs. Carl Schurtz in Watertown, Wisconsin and was taught in German. In 1860 the first English speaking kindergarten began in Boston and was founded by Elizabeth Peabody

Education for the Deaf

It must have been a breakthrough for the hearing impaired people to have their own means by which to communicate. **Abbe Charles Michel de l'Epee**, an ordained priest along with **Thomas Gallaudet**, and **Laurent Clerc** developed a sign language for use in schools in Paris in 1775. This was mainly the brainchild of Abbe Charles who had a strong desire for the deaf to hear the gospel of Jesus Christ. Later Thomas and Laurent brought the sign language to the USA where they opened a school for the deaf in Connecticut in 1817. As a result of this, deaf people are being educated and are able to assume normal employment.

Education for the Blind

There seems to be no evidence of education for the blind in the Old and New Testament. There was no mention of the blind except in the time of Christ where he miraculously restored the sight of some. In the 16th Century, attempts were made to teach the blind to read by using raised letters on wax or wood. It was in the first half of the 19th Century that **Louis Braille** accidentally lost his sight at the age of three and later became inspired by his father's carved images of Jesus to produce a method of reading for the blind. He had learned to read at a school for the blind in Paris that made use of Charles Barbier's method of elevated dots. This later became a motivating factor which inspired him to invent Braille.

Sunday Schools

In the time of the reformation Luther had encouraged education for all but this was not practical because children worked in factories and some parents did not see the need for their children to attend classes. Therefore, others like the poor and disadvantaged, did not learn to read or write. It was in 1780 when a committed Christian by the name of Robert Raikes of Scotland determined to help the children of the poor by teaching them the Bible on Sundays. His practice of Sunday school was rejected and resisted by many but some noble men of God like John and Charles Wesley, John Newton and many others came to his support, and the Sunday school movement was soon widely accepted spreading rapidly throughout Europe and the USA. After the enlightenment period during the 19th century when regulations prevented the teaching of the Bible in public schools in the USA, the Sunday school movement experienced rapid growth as parents resorted to them for instilling good Christian values in their children.

All of the above, had one common factor, that is, they originate due to an awareness of God based on knowledge of the Holy Scriptures. Thus, it can be said that many educational institutions, religious or secular, public or private is a visible reminder of the mandate of Jesus Christ.

Chapter Two

The Decline of Christian Education

2.1 Circumstances, People & Events Influencing Traditional Christian Education

In the preceding chapter various fundamentals of Christian education were highlighted. One very important observation is that the Bible was the foundation upon which all principles and methodology of Christian education was based. The curricula itself was theological which required a knowledge and understanding of the Holy Scriptures. However, as we approach the twentieth century, particularly after the renaissance period, significant changes began to take place in the area of Christian education. This transition came about as a result of scholars who were stimulated to explore and research other areas of philosophical thought. Emerging from these new interests, were a variety of idealism and dogmas. Some of these included modernism, pietism, liberalism and Secular Humanism, most of which influenced our societies, resulting in adverse effects upon the morals and values of Christian education. *"Significant changes have occurred in other national contexts giving rise to other new intellectual, political, economic and social philosophies. Some of these include the Enlightenment, the Industrial Revolution and increased urbanization and plurality."*[24]

The industrial revolution was a period of change where machines were invented. These machines were created to replace manual methods of manufacturing. The invention of machines came about as a result of the rapid production of raw materials. Industries such as coal, iron, steel, shipbuilding and textiles paved the way for the invention of machinery such as, ships, railways, engines and bridges. This revolution brought changes in the way people live and work and created an industrialized society. Prior to this, labour was manual however, there has been continuous advancement in manufacturing since that time.

Some other factors warranting change in the education system are modernism and liberalism.

> *"**Modernism** is a movement which developed in the 19th century in the Christian church to reconcile Christianity with science particularly the theory of evolution. This movement subjected the Bible to modern standards of study and literary criticism, interpreted dogmas in terms of modern philosophy and brought doctrine to the test of ethical and social significance. Pope Pius X in 1907 condemned Modernism because of its tendency to treat religion as a myth. This movement grew and became strong. In the USA there was an opposing movement called Fundamentalism brought about by Christians to preserve Christian philosophies. After 1930 there were new theological trends that avoided both extremes."*[25]

Liberalism is a term that is applied to social movements going as far back as the renaissance period. It is a social philosophy identified with the maximum freedom for individuals of all classes.

> *This movement had advanced into the 19th and 20th century among protestant circles that builds for the assumption that Christianity is reconcilable with the*

> *positive human aspiration, including the quest for autonomy. Liberalism desires to adapt religion to modern thought and culture. Consequently, it views divine love as realized primarily, if not totally, in love of one's neighbour and the kingdom of God as a present reality found especially within an ethically transformed society.*[26]

Religious Liberalism refers to the partial or complete freedom from clerical or traditional authority, favouring an individual's right to reject established dogmas. This was associated with the application of religious teaching to social problems. The Transcendental movement is an offshoot of Religious Liberalism.

Comenius 1592 – 1670 - German born Comenius was called "the first Modern Educator" and "The Prophet of Modern Education." "His education began late, at age 16, and he later studied at the University of Heidelberg. He had great concerns about the problems with education and became involved in Pastoral work as well as becoming the leader of a school in Moravia. He began writing while continuing his studies. The ever-promising future which seemed quite bright for Comenius suddenly grew dark as the cruelest of all religious conflicts occurred."[27] The year was 1618 when the thirty-day war began. Protestants, including political leaders and ministers, were jailed and executed. Catholicism was forced upon the population. Comenius escaped but this led him to plunge fully into the ministry, serving congregations in caves, huts, and other hiding places across the countryside. He continued writing pamphlets, tracts, homilies and books. Some of his books, the '*Didactic*', '*Labyrinth*' and '*Janua*' brought him great fame and he achieved celebrity status around the world. '*Janua*' was translated into sixteen languages with over a hundred editions.

Comenius believed in four kinds of schools.

1. *"The School of the Mother Knee"* representing the responsibility of the parents to train their children at home with emphasis on the scriptures.

2. *"The Vernacular School" involves a child learning the mother tongue rather than the classics. Of course, the arts and science would not be neglected during those elementary years.*

3. *"The Latin School" which focused on advance studies specializing in classical languages such as Greek Latin and Hebrew as well as science, literature and the arts.*

4. *"The School of University & Travel" for the genuine scholar who would be expected to make a contribution to the life of the church and the community. "Here leaders were created through original investigation and exploration of the ideals and morals of various nations. Comenius is generally credited with being the first to emphasize the educational significance of early childhood education."*[28]

Comenius believed that it was the social function of education to *reform society*. He was also innovative in his view of the teaching process. His textbooks, stressed the importance of action (*learning by doing*) which he viewed as the key to his system of learning. He utilized object lessons and pictures to stimulate a child's learning. He was also instrumental in writing the first textbook that applied pictures as a teaching device. He was not just a great contributor to education but also to Christianity in the area of reconciliation among churches and nations. Despite the many adverse circumstances in which he lived, he served the Lord faithfully and in obedience.

August Hermann Francke (1663 – 1727) - Francke grew up as a devoted Christian with an interest in gospel ministry. After private instructions, he attended the gymnasium at Gotha where he came under the influence of the philosophy of Comenius. His intellectual capabilities gained him entry at the University of Erfurt at age fourteen. He earned a degree at the University of Liepzig in 1685 and embarked on a teaching career. A few years later he withdrew himself from academic life in order to carry on private study and clarification of a personal philosophy of life and education. He accepted a position at the new University of Halle in Berlin in the Department of

Theology. *"The extent of Francke's educational ministry at Halle is almost unbelievable. Eby describes him as 'the noblest example of the practical education of Germany' and suggests that he may very well have been the most efficient representative of the Christian spirit in educational history."*[29] His achievement in Berlin include: opening the Elementary School of Glaucha for the education of the poor (1692), founding the orphan school (1695) which was supported by alms, the development of a school for teachers (1705), promoting a private boarding school for college preparation and a boarding house where students could lodge for free, establishing a publishing institute for biblical literature, opening an infirmary and a home for widows,. *"The University of Halle became the great Pietist centre supplying Europe with teachers, pastors, foreign missionaries and influential laymen."*[30]

Francke's teaching ideals stressed the aim of education as to honour God, and so his educational practice was based entirely on theological premises. He said all good instructions must combine godliness and wisdom which must be taught by living the knowledge of Christ in piety, prayer, Bible study and evangelism; and emphasized that all learning and knowledge is folly if it doesn't have as its foundation true and pure love toward God and man. He recognized the necessity for conversion and developed his educational programs around the concept that information about God's truth could bring students to the point of regeneration and build up their Christian faith.

He believed that all good students should be given the opportunity to learn, regardless of wealth or status and viewed the role of the teacher as an integral part of his educational system with emphasis on positive example. Love and discipline was important in the life of the teacher and profane words, derogatory names and ridicule were not appropriate for classroom use, as they were more harmful than good. It was said that teachers who graduated from Francke's schools were of higher calibre intellectually than other teachers.

He offered training for elementary school teachers who had to maintain some very rigid standards. These include moderate dress, temperate use of alcohol and tobacco, a serious commitment to teaching and an affectionate patience with children. Although the standards were rigid, no teacher would violate those principles.

His curriculum was permeated by the Holy Scriptures which formed the core for all levels of instruction. He used scriptures to formally explain truth. He believed that by applying these scriptures to the hearts and consciences of his pupils, they would in turn teach these same truths to others. In other words, scripture formed the basis of his curriculum.

His educational goals include a strong emphasis on Christian living. He had hoped that through the power of education at all levels of society; evil would eventually be eradicated from the world. At Halle University, he was busy reforming the theological curriculum while developing the curriculum in his children's schools and teacher's colleges. Theological students received free board and lodging for 4-6 years and were required to read the Old and New Testament and write commentaries on each of the books in the Bible.

Francke's influence on Christian education up to the present time is virtually immeasurable. The impact of Halle University resulted in a similar pattern adopted in John's Hopkins University which was founded in Baltimore, Maryland in 1867.

2.2 The Enlightenment

The eighteenth century ushered in another philosophical movement known as the Enlightenment. This was characterized by rationalism and provided a stimulus for learning.

> *The enlightenment is a term used to describe a way of thought which became common among the educated classes. The term is also used to describe the ferment and spread of ideas and implies that reason, not passion should direct thought and that reason should replace prejudice and superstition.*[31]

One of the great advocates of this movement was **Frances Bacon** (1561 – 1626) who placed great emphasis on the statement

"***Knowledge is power***" and his scientific ideals of an objective methodical investigation of nature. The philosophy behind this movement is that man and society could be brought to a state of perfection. Francis Bacon taught that the scriptures were foundational to science and art.

Born in Ilchester England, he studied at Oxford and Paris where he received his doctor of Theology degree. In his most important work '*Opus Majus*', he pointed out the need to study science and nature as subjects at school. This work was in itself an encyclopedia of scientific topics and teaching instructions. It was Bacon who predicted the invention of the aero plane, the submarine and the automobile.

France was the centre of the enlightenment for it was there that many of the outstanding thinkers met in salons to discuss their latest ideas. It was here also that writers would test their views before publishing their own works. Never before had the world seen so many students, even the working class was motivated toward study. There was an outburst of scientific thought in the seventeenth century. From this stemmed many great scientists like the American Patriot Benjamin Franklin with his invention in the area of electricity. Many books were also published during this time.

The enlightenment was a contributing factor in changing the pattern of American education. This was due mainly to the rationalism of Rene Descartes (1596 – 1650) and the emphasis on human education. From here on we begin to see a shift away from the Christian faith as man was to be studied as they did nature, and therefore man became explainable through natural laws. Christianity, as a result of this, was being ridiculed mainly as a violation of natural law.

Constitutional Changes in the USA

In the USA, constitutional changes produced a separation of Church and State which paved the way towards secular education. This new legislation prevented conveying of any form of religion through the curriculum of the public schools. The State therefore gained influence, authority and control over the education system. The

Enlightenment was successful in shifting the focus of education to a non-biblical perspective of teaching, concentrating mainly on science, history and the arts. This was followed by further legislation that prohibited any religious education, Bible reading and prayer in public schools. Strong Christian values were pushed aside and Christian educators lost their influence on public education. This gave rise to the secular voice of the Enlightenment.

The enlightenment set ablaze the fire of humanistic influence. Humanists were quick to realize the battle for one's mind could be won or lost through reading and education. Therefore, the philosophies of humanism were communicated into the minds of students through the teaching of art, fiction, plays, poetry, etc. Although the humanistic elements had surfaced during the renaissance, the enlightenment paved the way for rapid growth and further influence. Two great advocates of this movement were the French philosopher, Voltaire (1694-1778) and Rousseau (1712-1778). *"Voltaire produced eighty three volumes of books, pamphlets and plays that swept through France and Southern Europe."*[32]

The fire of humanistic ideals continued to burn through books and education in Europe and the USA. Students' thoughts were affected, and controlled, some of whom later became teachers and continued the trend of humanistic influence up to the 21st century.

The American civil war (1861-1865) set the stage for the acceptance of humanism. The minds of people were affected, causing them to become vulnerable and receptive to new ideologies. Charles Darwin had just published his book *"The Origins of the Species"* (1859). In this book, Darwin outlined his theory of evolution that man's existence could be explained by nature rather than supernatural means. This also placed emphasis on man's natural abilities rather than the supernatural ability of God.

It was during this time that religionists became Pietists, focusing only on their inner self and personal devotion. Meanwhile, humanism had subtly entered the educational system and was becoming the accepted norm while religious thinkers made very little effort to refute it.

2.3 Secular Humanism & the Curriculum (in the U.S.A.)

> *The 19th century marked the beginning of secular education. Until that time the schools were all church-related. Horace Mann in the early 1800 spearheaded the beginning of the first public school. This move was actually motivated by Hegelian philosophy, which holds that man's ideas were superior to biblical principles. Public schools at the time were still influenced greatly by biblical thought but this was the beginning of a plan to change the emphasis in education from religious concepts to humanistic concepts.*[33]

Since Secular Humanism has greatly affected Christian education, it is important that we focus briefly on the subject.

Jim L Smith, quoted Corliss Lamont as saying:

> *...Humanism is the viewpoint that men have but one life to lead and should make the most of it in terms of creative work and happiness; that human happiness is its own justification and requires no sanction or support from supernatural sources; that, in any case the supernatural, usually conceived of in the form of heavenly gods or immortal heavens, does not exist; and that human beings, using their own intelligence and cooperating liberally with one another, can build an enduring citadel of peace and beauty upon this earth.*[34]

The basic tenets of Secular Humanism are:

Atheism: The belief that there is no God

Evolution: The theory that all existing life today originated from a primeval, non-created single life-form through chance or natural selection and that the universe itself is the result of chance development rather than creation.

Amorality: If man evolved from animal he may as well behave like one, e.g. if it feels good do it.

Autonomy: Man is autonomous, the highest of all life form and there is no God to answer to. They believe that each individual can solve his own problem and make moral decisions independent of any Supreme Being.

Communist Worldview: A one world Socialist State would solve the world's problem, this is suggested in global interdependence, international democracy and universal society, etc.

Dr Paul Kurtz in regards to Humanism says, "...There is an influential philosophical tradition that maintains that ethics is an autonomous field of inquiry, that ethical judgments can be formulated independently of revealed religion, and that human beings can cultivate practical reason and wisdom and by its application achieve lives of virtue and excellence..."[35]

> *Actually the fountainhead of humanist curriculum began in 1918 when the National Education Association (NEA) initiated its Seven Cardinal Principles that emphasized humanist ethical values."[36] The shift in educational trends continues with the establishment of the National Education Association. "Dr. James Kennedy quotes Dr. John Goodland of the NEA in his report to the NEA entitled "Schooling For The Future" as saying, "Our goal is behavioral change. The majority of our youth still hold to the values of their parents and if we do not recognize this pattern, if we do not re-socialize them to accept change, out society may decay. Dr. Goodland went on to say that the goal of the NEA is that of changing children from the traditional values of their parents. In other words, the traditional parental views*

on morals must be replaced by individual autonomy in decision-making."[37] They argue that "many children still hold to the values of their parents and their educational strategies are to re-socialize them to accept change otherwise the society might decay.[38]

Such behavioral change is expected to come about through educational methods and in the material used in schools' curriculum. Some of the terms used in reference to their objectives are; values changing, values clarification, self actualizing, value indicating, values teaching, morals education, human development programs and values education.

The Effects of Secular Humanism on Public Schools (USA)

A study investigating the content of 1,291 American school readers show a sharp decrease in the amount of moral and religious concepts in the materials used in public schools. This will be seen in the chart below:[39]

Time Period	Percentage in moral content & Religious Education
1776 –1786	100%
1788 –1825	50% (Decline)
1825 – 1880	21% (Decline)
1916 - 1920	5% (Decline)
1920 - Present	So small basically immeasurable

American, **John Dewey** was considered "the father of progressive education". He was born in 1859 in Vermont. He was influenced by certain philosophical ideas as well as by individuals such a Johann H. Pestalozzi (1746-1827), Johann F. Herbert (1778 – 1841), Friedrich Froebel (1782 – 1852) among others.

To a large extent, Dewey is responsible for the demise of religious instructions in the American schools. He disliked Christianity and the dividing of mankind into "saved" and "unsaved". He felt this created a road-block to progressive education. With this kind of conviction, he was determined to eradicate Christianity. Dewey earned his Ph.D. at Johns Hopkins University in 1884. His philosophy includes *"a worship of science, a belief in the inherent goodness of man, the rejection of absolutes and fixed truth with no genuine goals for education outside of the individual and his society but rather sinister political implications."*[40]

As the ideologies of Secular Humanism became rampant in America, Europe and other regions of the world, so the changes in curriculum became obvious, prompting many heated battles between humanists and Christians. Sex education was among the subjects included in the curriculum. This was taught in a negative sense where premarital sex was promoted. This in turn gave rise to premarital sex and other sexually immoral activities among school age children.

An association called Sex Information and Education Council of the United States, (SIECUS) was organized by Dr. Mary Calderon in 1964. In a lecture at a pre-teen boys' school she said *"sex is for fun and gives a wonderful sensation, it is not just something that married people do in bed in the dark in one position.* She said *"children must learn how to use sex"*[41].

2:4 The New Age Movement and the World Core Curriculum.

The New Age Movement and associated organizations like the **United Nations** have also influenced education. **Robert Muller** – former assistant Secretary General of the United Nations have designed what is called the "World Core Curriculum for Global Education" as a result of this he was awarded the UNESCO Prize for Peace Education in 1989. This curriculum is now been tested in The Robert Muller Schools as well as other schools. *"The underlying philosophy upon which The Robert Muller School is based will be* *found in the teachings set forth in the books of Alice Bailey,"*[42] says Robert Muller.

Alice Bailey was born in Manchester, England 16th June, 1880. She was raised in an orthodox Christian family but said she grew up very unhappy. At the age of fifteen she had a visitation by an "Ascended Master". She migrated to the USA where many other visitations followed but her main spirit guide was (Djwhal Khul) who inspired her to write many books. *"Alice Bailey spent most of her time working on something she called, "The Plan" the results of which gave birth to many New Age groups such as: The Church Universal and Triumphant, Benjamin Crème's The Tara Centre, the Robert Muller Schools and the Temple of Understanding, to name a few."*[43] These and many other organizations continue to be influenced by Alice Bailey's work.

The World Core Curriculum is seen as a revolution in education which prepares students to be cooperative planetary citizens, the basis upon which a new world can emerge. It has as its basic platform the value of the individual and his/her unique place in the "One Humanity". Students are empowered to be aware of themselves as "cosmic units" and one with the whole of humankind. *"In spite of ourselves, we have become a "global village", and we are inextricably interconnected in all dimensions."*[44]

The curriculum reflects this universality of life in the concept of The Four Harmonies on which Dr. Muller based his system. These are:[45]

1) ***Our Planetary Home and Place in the Universe*** – this deals with planet earth and its relation to the universe and includes stars, outer space and the entire biosphere, embracing microbiology and genetics as well as the area of nuclear physics.

2) ***Our Human Family*** – this deals with the various human groups, teaches about beauty and the meaning of diversity which include unity and a sense of oneness for world peace.

3) ***Our Place In Time*** – reveals vast evolutionary development

4) ***The Miracle of Individual Human Life*** – this brings to education the idea of the uniqueness of the individual, the miracle of life and true human fulfillment in this planetary experience. Students will become "right servers of the planet and universe".

The following chart has been prepared to summarize the various changes and developments in Christian education throughout the ages:

2.5 Chart Highlighting Educational Trends Throughout the Ages

The Ages	Teacher/Instructor	Setting	Curriculum	Methodology	Students
O/T Pre-flood era, 4000 B.C.	God	Garden Of Eden	Creation & Nature	Oral instructions	Adam & Eve
2000 – 1500 B.C.	God	Mt. Sinai	Building pattern for Tabernacle	Oral Instructions	Moses
1440 B.C.	God, Moses, Parents, Rabbis Prophets, Priests, Levites	Wilderness, home & Synagogues	The Law & Torah	Memorization, reading & oral instructions	Jews (all ages)
N/T 4th Century	Jesus, Apostles, parents Rabbis	Synagogues, seaside, mountains homes, Christian homes	Holy Scriptures & the Law	Parables, questioning, word pictures	Jesus' Disciples, Followers of The Way, Gentiles, whosoever
Middle Ages 500 –1300	Minister, Church leaders, Roman Catholics, Priests	Church/home Schools, Synagogue, Monastic & Cathedral schools	Scriptures Catechumens, Didache, Apostles creed	Reading, drama memorization, writing, worship &	Christians, scholars of theology, intellectuals
Renaissance 1400-1600	Church Leaders & Roman Catholics, Priests, Ministers	Home, Church Schools, Churches	Scriptures Catechumens, Didache, Apostles creed, Humanities, science, Art & Languages	Reading, memorization, writing, worship & drama & interpretation	Christians, Scholars of theology
Reformation 1500-1800	Church Leaders & Roman Catholics, Private teachers, Ministers	The Church, Learned Scholars	Scriptures Catechumens, Didache, Apostles creed, Humanities, science, Art & Languages	Lecturers, Hands on, Research, Writing Memorization, Drama & Worship	Students of all social standing, Intellectuals, Christians
Enlightenment 1800	Intellectuals, Writers, Lecturers, Teachers, Clergy, Professors, Ministers	Salons, Private Schools, Colleges, Universities	Science, Humanities, Languages, Religion,	Lectures, discussions, Audio Visuals, etc.	Students of all social standing.

2.6 *Observations*

1. Prior to the Middle Ages and even up until the time of the renaissance, education was significantly influenced by the Holy Scriptures. The foundation was laid by God at creation in instructions to Adam and Eve, then to Moses and the prophets. Jesus continued these principles by teaching the Scriptures and instructed his disciples to do likewise, a task they took seriously resulting in the rapid spread of Christianity.

2. The period of the renaissance brought many changes to the pattern of education when other schools of thoughts and ideas presented new avenues of learning and fields of exploration. The scope of education was no longer limited to theology and related studies but broadened to include art, science, humanities languages and architecture, etc.

3. Then came the time of the Enlightenment that paved the way for even further explosion of knowledge. Scientific discoveries brought about the invention of machinery creating new industries. Many new ideals developed during this period of the enlightenment and the humanists discovered that the battle for ones mind could be won through teaching. It is during this time that a significant twist in Christian education began – less God and more of man.

4. In this quest for knowledge, Christianity and its religious morals were sacrificed. This was replaced by the many new philosophies that were developed during the enlightenment. Among these philosophies was humanism, emphasizing the study of man and nature rather than God. The curriculum of the public schools was no longer based on God and the Holy Scriptures but was made secular in all aspects. This is portrayed in principles such as that of *no absolutes* "no right or wrong" and man was basically in charge of himself with no Supreme Being to give account to. The curriculum was used as the vehicle to convey these ideals. Failure of the church to carry out

the educational mandate resulted in the emergence of secular schools.

5. Since the World Core Curriculum has been endorsed by the United Nations for Global Education, further curriculum changes are envisioned when this becomes mandatory for public school education. Children are being targeted for the spread of New Age philosophy and New Agers see no better way than to infiltrate the education system.

One can now make the following conclusion:

a) Christian education has definitely declined from the fundamentals of the past.

b) The Bible is no longer recognized as the essential authority for instruction, doctrine and practice in the public school system.

c) There is a major problem with the present educational system. These problems must be addressed by Christian educators in the interest of our children and future generations.

Chapter Three

Rekindling the Flame of Christian Education

"Education is not filling a pail but the lighting of a fire"
William Butler Yeats, Irish poet and dramatist

3.1 Rekindle the Flame!

We have established that there has been significant decline in the biblical standards of education. Responsibility to educate lies in the hands of government or state operated institutions in most cases, therefore the church has lost the ability to control or influence the educational systems. This chapter discusses ways of **rekindling the flame of Christian education.**

In the earlier chapters it was shown that teaching was at the very heart of God and he emphasized its importance when he instructed Moses in Deuteronomy chapter 6. Moses was to ensure that knowledge of God and his requirements of mankind were passed down to all generations though his teaching. The Israelites were thus instructed and were expected to learn and understand the meaning and implication of the Laws of God. They were also expected to obey the commands of God by applying his Laws to their personal lives.

Christianity brought certain benefits to biblical education. We can see the hand of God at work in scripture as he reveals himself to us from Genesis to Revelation. From the inception of the early church, Christians (disciples of Jesus Christ) were commissioned by him in Matt 28:19-20 to teach the scriptures to all nations. Consequently, the only people with the God given responsibility of teaching the Holy Scriptures are the Christians, meaning Christians are held accountable to God to carry out this mandate.

3.2 Secular School vs. Christian School

Society in general has been adversely affected by a subsequent decline in morals and ethical values. The absence of strong biblical principles in the curriculum of secular schools and colleges is the main contributor to escalating crime rate, immoral lifestyles, and sub-standard academic performance among high school and college students.

Christian schools have placed great spiritual emphasis on their curriculum ensuring that it includes learning experiences which serve as good examples to the student. It helps to develop strong principles and concepts about biblical truths while endorsing the belief in God as creator of the universe and all in it. Prayer is another component of the Christian school system. Prayer enables the students to focus and direct petitions to Almighty God thereby developing a relationship with him as well as an allegiance to him. Christian morals and character are developed as the Christian education touches the tri-part unit of the student: a) Body – physical education, b) soul and mind – intellectual textbook application, c) spirit – the Holy Bible inspired by God becomes practical through the Holy Spirit.

Characteristics of the Christian school

1. It helps each student see the world through the lens of biblical truths.

2   It acquaints the students with the world by way of the general study of natural science, social studies and other studies which deal with proper biblical and ethical human relationships.

3   It prepares the student for intelligent and satisfactory living, enabling them to take their place in society as good representatives of the Christian faith.

4   It guides students in making appropriate vocational choices.

The curriculum of Christian education includes liberal arts and sciences, usually sub-divided into the humanities, social sciences and the natural sciences. The objective of the curriculum is two-fold, i.e., to teach vocational expertise necessary for employment as well as to develop the students' spiritually so that they can pursue their lives of faith in obedience to God and his specific laws.

Students attending Christian schools are exposed to certain disciplines, which cultivate feelings and imagination and also expand the mind through biblical concepts and other subjects such as art, literature, history and science. Christian schools differ in that they maintain that students are more than just computerized numbers in a group. Instead, students are treated as people with feelings and emotion and are seen as special and unique to God and their teacher.

In essence, in the Christian schools the students learn:

1.   The Bible as the main textbook, the manual for their lives,

2.   God is the creator of the universe and all living things therein,

3.   Each individual has a soul which needs to respond to God,

4.   The 3 R's (Reading Writing and Arithmetic) as well as other subjects of importance,

5.   To respect and give keen attention to their teachers

6.   It is not right morally to cheat on test or homework

7. The value of honouring and respecting their parents and to honour their promises. Basically do what they said they would do, respectfully.

8. To perform well whatever task is assigned to them at home, school or in the workplace.

The responsibility of Christian schools is to offer a very high standard of Christian education inclusive of excellent academic programs suitable for the development of all of the faculties, spiritually, mentally, socially and physically. Therefore the balance between academic excellence and sound biblical teaching is the main objective of Christian education in the Christian school. The ultimate goal of the Christian school is to lead the students to recognize Jesus Christ as their Lord and Saviour.

Statistics through evaluation and testing have proven that those who pursue their education at Christian schools receive a far superior standard of education.

The secular schools

The secular school system is influenced by the philosophies of Secular Humanism and other non-Christian ideals which are conveyed through the curriculum. This includes teaching atheistic and evolutionary principles which in turn produces skeptics, atheists and agnostics as by-products of ungodly influences.

Educational emphasis in secular schools is geared at the academic aspect. Students are being prepared for vocational and professional employment while the spiritual aspect is neglected, leaving them ill-equipped to face life's challenges. Immorality is promoted in a very subtle way. Textbooks and other required reading materials endorse violence, witchcraft, Satanism, sexual immorality, etc.

The absence of moral and theological content in the curriculum of the secular schools has resulted in biblical illiteracy. **Biblical Illiteracy** has caused great concern among many Christians. Even in some evangelical churches, very little emphasis is placed on teaching that which is biblical, factual or doctrinal in content. The Christian community is not thoroughly furnished or exposed to biblical teaching, doctrinal understanding or ethical principles to be able to defend the faith. Instead, this lack of biblical knowledge has caused believers to become vulnerable to cults and other non-Christian organizations.

Society is also presented with the problem of the breakdown of morals and ethical values among employees in the workplace, students in schools and colleges and even among those who professes the Christian faith.

Church and school once worked together as a team complementing and supporting each other in teaching biblical standards and concepts. The Bible was the very fibre that held together people of all social standing. Now, educational criteria has shifted away from what God had originally intended. The curriculum communicates hidden philosophies destined to change the minds of the learners from beliefs and morals inherited from parents and faith groups. For example, in the U.S.A., what is being taught in secular schools rests heavily in the hands of humanistic controlled organizations such as the State, the government, the education boards or other organizations such as the National Education Association (NEA), The American Library Association (ALA), and Sex Information and Education Council of the United States (SIECUS).

Grant R. Jeffrey made the following observations:

> *Teachers from kindergarten and up are attending seminars on professional development days to learn how to teach your child to enter a trance state and explore occult visualization. Astral travel, experiments in clairvoyance, and dream interpretation are commonly offered to elementary children without their parents' knowledge or approval. School boards and teachers fight with all their ability to prevent any Christian or biblical influence within the school under the spurious argument of "Separation of Church and State." However, these same teachers and boards are actively*

promoting New Age and Hindu religious beliefs disguised as meditation.[46]

3.3 Why Christian Education?

Often times the question is asked, "Why should one pay expensive tuition for Christian education when public school education is of little or no cost at all?"

In answering this question, one must first determine their intended expectation from an educational experience, taking into consideration the fact that education is the foundation to the future of any learner and such education will determine the quality of one's life. Belief systems or philosophies, will, to a great extent determine the way people live. For example, if our educational system portrays deception or anything contrary to God's truth, then it is likely that our students will develop lifestyles devoid of moral and godly principles; lifestyles that will wreck havoc in the society resulting in serious consequences on their lives and on the society at large. Therefore, the outcome of the learner, is considerably determined by the system of education.

The basis of any education system largely depends on the philosophy of the institution or school, namely what the school or institution believes. There are two basic beliefs: a) **Naturalism** where the system of education does not acknowledge the existence of God. Instead, they accept and teach the evolution theory that *"all existing life forms originate from a primeval, non-created single life-form through chance or natural selection and that the universe is a result of chance development."*[47] b) **Creationism** where the school or institution acknowledges and believes in God as creator of all living beings, such education promotes a life of faith and obedience to Him. Therefore every school or institution of learning has in place a **Philosophy of Education**.

Dr. Denton Rhone in an article entitled *"Who is Educating your Child?"* explains it way, *"There are three elements in each philosophy of education. These elements are needed to have a proper philosophy of education. These are metaphysics, Axiology and Epistemology.*

Metaphysics has to do with your understanding of reality – what is real.

Axiology has to do with the question of values – what is right or what is wrong?

Epistemology has to do with your understanding of truth – what is truth? Who defines truth?"[48]

In the Christian school, the metaphysics would be the acknowledgement of the existence of God as the creator of every living thing. The Axiology of the Christian school (concept of right and wrong) would be determined by the doctrines and principles of the Bible. The epistemology of the Christian school (the question of what is truth) will be conveyed by the fact that God is the source of all truth. This truth is revealed to us in the Bible which guides reason, intuition and the senses. Hence the Bible forms the basis of all authority. The basis for Christian education is scriptural as seen in Is. 54:13 *"All thy children shall be taught of the Lord."*

3.4 A Christian Based Curriculum

> *"The word "curriculum" is derived from a Latin word meaning "a place of running; a race course"; a course of study, therefore, a line of progress through a series of subjects. In its broadest meaning, the curriculum includes all activities and experience which are initiated or utilized by the church or school for the accomplishment of the aims of Christian education." A narrower meaning refers to the curriculum as "areas or fields of subject matter organized into learning areas."*[49]

Some other definitions of curriculum are as follows:

1. *"Curriculum is the organization of learning activities guided by a teacher with the intent of changing behaviour."*[50]

2. *"Generally, curriculum includes both the materials and the experiences for learning. Specifically, curriculum is the written courses of study used for Christian education."*[51]

The curriculum will be influenced by the Christian view of education and the philosophy of the school. The general objective of any curriculum is to combine Christian content and experience in order to train the hearts and minds of the learner in God's truth and produce transformed lives. Robert W. Pazmiño says:

> *"No simple formula to accomplish an adequate blending of content and experience exist, but certain guidelines can be shared. The teacher is called to be knowledgeable and sensitive to dimensions of the content and to the various experiences of the students within their particular context. Through this Knowledge and sensitivity, a teacher can tailor the presentation of materials to the needs of the students. This blending implies complimentary concerns for truth and love in a Christian worldview along with a host of Christian virtues that teachers seek to model."*[52]

The curriculum will therefore determine:

1) what should be taught (subject - material, principle, concept or value)

2) why should these areas be taught (goals and behavioral objectives)

3) where is the teaching being done (setting - must be conducive to learning),

4) how is the teaching to be done (methodology – teaching methods)

5) when should various areas be taught (chronological age & spiritual maturity)

6) who is being taught (know the students background and personal details)

7) who is teaching (the teacher must have the required qualification and meet all other criteria)

8) what organizing principles holds it all together (philosophy based on biblical principles)

The following information give some guidelines in developing an effective curriculum[53]

Curriculum Guide for Christian Education

The curriculum guide provides users with purposeful guidelines and information relating to the nature of the areas to be covered in the curriculum such as the content and methodology organized in appropriate sequence for each age group in conjunction with the overall goals of the school. The basic components of the curriculum guide are as follows:

1. It must contain a brief statement of the general philosophy of the school

2. It presents a chart or other device that indicates the scope of the curriculum in terms of subject matter to the taught, concept to be developed, mental process to be utilized, or a combination of all three.

3. It includes a statement presenting how the scope is sequenced

4. It contains statement of objectives that are provided for the overall planned curriculum program, for each unit and for each lesson. They are stated in observable and/or measurable student performance descriptors to enable the teacher to monitor learner outcomes

5. It suggests appropriate education media for use in the instructional program as the teacher or teaching team will not be able to keep up with the increasing volume of teaching resources. Specialists in instructional media can examine, test and suggest effective new media to be listed in the curriculum guide.

6. It includes provisions for evaluation. Formative and summative evaluation components should be included. These provide the teacher with the following:

    a) Instruments and procedures to maintain the continuous feedback of corrective information to learners.

    b) Valid and reliable means of assessing the terminal output of the program

    c) pre-teaching diagnostic techniques and instruments

Curriculum Design in Christian Education

In the book "Modern Elementary Curriculum", Hilda Taba suggested the following 7-step sequence in designing the curriculum:[54]

1. Diagnostic of needs
2. Formulation of objectives
3. Selection of content
4. Organization of content
5. Selection of learning experiences
6. Organization of learning experiences
7. Determination of what to evaluate

However, rather than reinventing, one may take advantage of the many pre-designed Christian education based curriculum that are readily available. Two of the most popular ones are as follows:

1. Abeka – A traditional teacher-centred textbook approach for grades K –12

2. ACE (Accelerated Christian Education) students are motivated toward self instruction thus requiring minimal supervision.

H. W. Byrne suggests the following as good curriculum theory:[55]

1. The curriculum should be Christ centred and controlled by his Holy Spirit

2. People related graded to the need of pupil and psychological laws applied Bible integrated

3. Unified in purpose and content

4. Seek to develop personality in its fullest, physically, socially and spiritually

5. Well organized so that the sequence provides themes of seasonal interest units of study cumulative interest.

6. Should be evangelist, seeking to bring all ages to a knowledge of Jesus Christ as Saviour and Lord

7. Provide attractive practical materials of high quality.

In developing a curriculum, one must also take into consideration the mission and purpose of the institution. However, the above information can serve as a guide to those who prefer to develop their own curriculum, tailored to the needs of the institution with definite behavioral objectives in mind.

Recently there have been new approaches to curriculum development. Education reformers are moving away from what was considered the traditional textbook approach to developing curriculum that provides innovative learning experiences.

3.5 The Role of a Teacher of Christian Education

Teaching is a divine calling which is identified among the five-fold ministries in Eph 4:11-12, *"for the edifying and building up"*. The word 'teach' comes from the Anglo Saxon word *taecean* meaning "to show how to do". The teacher's role is an important one, that of ministry. It was recognized as a sacred responsibility and similar to that of the rabbis in Jewish synagogues. Although under the umbrella of a pastor, the teacher, when serving in the capacity of class teacher, is to assume the role of shepherd of those students, similar to the responsibilities of the pastor.

The teacher's life should therefore reflect godly character in example, having a desire for the salvation of souls, regularly attending church, exercising self denial and maintaining an active prayer life and personal devotion time. Additionally, the teacher should be an avid reader of the Bible and other materials related to teaching and must actively pursue further knowledge including that of current events. The teacher must have the knowledge of classroom management and administration to efficiently perform expected duties.

Words associated with teaching are helping, awakening, imparting, inspiring, correcting, sharing and guiding. Jesus Christ demonstrated all these qualities. Christian teaching is an art, which demands time, careful preparation and sacrifice.

The main duty of the Christian educator is to reveal God and be a witness through real life example demonstrating Christ-likeness through verbal expressions of truth concerning the nature of God and the truth of him. *"As an educator, the Christian teacher functions in accordance with the mandate of God to teach and in the whole educational and pedagogical principles contained in the entire* educative process. In this regard the teacher becomes an oracle of God (I Pet 4:10-11). This makes the teacher God's mouthpiece."[56]

A successful teacher must be knowledgeable in areas such as:

1. Knowledge of the Lord – this is first-hand experiential knowledge
2. Knowledge of the Bible – The textbook of Christian educators
3. Knowledge of related subjects such as biblical archeology, geography and history
4. Knowledge of the students – some background information and personal details
5. Knowledge of teaching techniques
6. Knowledge of classroom administration

The following quote places great emphasis on the importance of teaching:

> *The education of Crown Prince Akihito was a spectacle to all who had the confidence of the Imperial Family. His uncle, Senior Prince Takamatau, described it. The peerage took charge of the young prince, subjecting him to the most rigid discipline. Since he was one day to ascend the throne, he was to be taught the things that an emperor must know. More than that, he was not to be just any emperor – over some small island or backward country. This was the future emperor of Japan, with his country's own peculiar needs to consider. Our task is much the same, except that it is an infinitely higher work, requiring a more inspired discipline and a knowledge and wisdom that measures with the mind of God, the Emperor of the universe. Our curricula at all levels, then, must measure with his standard.*[57]

John Milton Gregory in his Book "The Seven Laws of Teaching"[58] highlighted seven factors that are present in every instance of true teaching which he considers the leading principles and rules of the art of teaching. These are as follows:

1. **The Law of the Teacher – Preparation**: A teacher must be prepared in knowledge by knowing the lesson content thoroughly and be able to communicate effectively that knowledge for successful teaching results. This preparation includes personal study of lesson content, careful selection of teaching materials, thorough planning of teaching process, and adept selection of teaching methods and thorough development of teaching procedures.

2. **The law of the student** – the student must attend with interest to the material being taught. The teacher should be able to keep the students interest aroused, thereby causing him to maintain attention. Proper planning and teaching methods will take care of this.

3. **The Law of the Language** – Language must be common to both teacher and student. New words must be explained and pronounced properly and communication must be clearly articulated. Encourage classroom discussions.

4. **The law of the lesson** – the truth to be taught must be connected to truth already known. Jesus practiced this when he taught new truths in light of that which was already familiar. For examples his parables include characters such as The Shepherd, The Sower, Ten Virgins all related to the times in which they lived.

5. **The Law of the teaching process** – The teacher's function is to motivate and guide the pupil. In so doing the teacher awakens and sets in motion the mode of the student, arousing his self-activities. This will cause the learner to acquire the knowledge by self-learning.

6. **The Law of the Learning process** – The student's response to the teacher's efforts. Gregory noted that there are five steps in the learning process; these are: memorization, understanding, expressing the thought, and giving evidence for beliefs and application of knowledge in daily life.

7. **The Law of Review and Application** – This demands that the completion, test and confirmation of the work of the teacher must be made by review and application. Reviewing evaluates both the teaching and learning process but also reinforces knowledge.

Becoming a "good" teacher is a life long developmental journey that includes self-discovery and self-mastery. The quality of teaching required is teaching that flows out of our spiritual beings. This depends on knowledge of Christ and our daily relationship with him. It does not depend on our intellectual accomplishments or technical skills but on our relationship with the Master teacher. It is only that relationship that will cause us to become passionate, dependable, knowledgeable, serving in humility and love for the spiritual, physical and social development of our learners.

Paul in the book of Titus, provide some very interesting insights in relation to teaching which is quite an appropriate way to end this section on the teacher's role.

> *You must teach what is in accord with sound doctrine. Teach the older men to be temperate, worthy of respect, self-control, and sound in faith, in love and in endurance. Likewise, teach the older women to be reverent in the way they live, not to be slanderers or addicted to much wine, but to teach what is good. Then they can train the younger women to love their husbands and children to be self-controlled and pure, to be busy at home, to be kind, and to be subject to their husbands, so that no one will malign the Word of God. Similarly, encourage the young men to be self-controlled. In everything set them as an example by*

doing what is good. In your teaching show integrity, seriousness and soundness of speech that cannot be condemned, so that those who oppose you may be ashamed because they have nothing bad to say about us. Teach slaves to be subject to their masters in everything, to try to please them, not to talk back to them, and not to steal from them, but to show that they can be fully trusted, so that in everyway they will make the teaching about God our Saviour attractive.

For the grace of God that brings salvation has appeared to all men. It teaches us to say "no" to ungodliness and worldly passions and to live self-controlled upright and godly lives in this present age, while we wait for the blessed hope – the glorious appearing of our God and Saviour, Jesus Christ, who gave himself for us to redeem us from all wickedness and to purify for himself a people that are his very own, eager to do what is good. These, then, are the things you should teach. Encourage and rebuke with all authority. Do not let anyone despise you." (Titus 2 1-15) (NIV)

3.6 Teaching Methods for the Christian School

Present teaching methods focus on memory resulting in underdevelopment of the other mental faculties. Traditional methods of teaching were largely teacher-centred. The teacher did the work of preparing thoroughly by studying and planning with the hope of capturing and holding the attention of the learner. The teacher is also expected to do everything from preparation to verbally expounding of the lesson. The learners listen with very little participation or activity. Newer creative approaches to learning involve the teacher guiding the students toward effective learning activities. Teachers use a number of teaching methods to involve the students in the learning process and students in turn learn by discovery.

Teaching methods depends on the objectives of the teaching and learning process. They must match content and students' needs. This means the different learning abilities among the learners must be taken into consideration. The most effective teaching methods are those that incorporate educational exercises which touch all five senses. This is called active learning, and has been adopted in some Sunday schools programmes. Experts of Education are finding that active learning is much more effective than the traditional workbook and story telling norm. An example of this is the Hands-On-Bible Curriculum, which is considered to be a revolutionary approach to learning. Students utilize a learning lab with a lot of colourful gizmos – things to touch, see, feel, smell and hear all pertaining to the lesson.

In active learning, students are given the opportunity to become actively involved in the learning process by hands-on group participation. Students are intrigued and maintain interest resulting in the ability to learn and retain more and use knowledge more effectively. The teacher becomes supervisor of the learning process, guiding the students by debriefing and encouraging discussions to ensure that the main point, truth or moral, has been driven home to the students.

Comenius, a great contributor to education, emphasized many years ago that students learn better by doing or by direct experience. Traditional curricular methods need reforming to incorporate teaching methods that are more effective. It means incorporating those teaching methods that offer greater results. We need to adopt the "less is better" approach where less material is covered in more detail with more care. Sometimes we waste too much time lecturing detailed materials to which the learner have difficulty relating, retaining or applying.

3.7 Lessons from the Master Teacher

Christian educators must take note of the pattern set by Jesus in order to successfully carry out his mandate to make disciples. Jesus was referred to as a "teacher" approximately forty five times.

1. Mark 1:21-22 tells us Jesus' teaching was authoritative. He was the revelation of God and his life authenticated his work as teacher.

2. His teaching methods were not that of an authoritarian meaning he did not impose his teaching upon his hearers. We see this in John 6:60-69.

3. Jesus' teaching encouraged thinking. This we see in his personal communication with his hearers. The teacher should refrain from providing answers and instead utilize open-ended question that will arouse curiosity and thinking.

4. Jesus lived what he taught; his life demonstrated his love for all humanity – love, a subject that was stressed so much in his teaching.

5. His teaching was oral instructions, similar to the oral traditions of the Hebrew people in the Old Testament. Although it is said that oral instructions results in only 10% retention, Jesus applied certain factors that made his method of teaching effective. This can be attributed to the way he used word pictures and other colourful illustrations, utilizing themes with which his hearers were familiar. His teachings usually focus on their needs.

6. His teaching was spontaneous with simplicity and sensitivity which explains Deut 6 where the importance of seizing a teachable moment is illustrated. One was expected to teach anywhere, anytime and anyone regardless of age or social standing.

7. Jesus' teaching was contextualized. This means applying and adapting truth to specific contexts of situations. His teaching was tailored to his audience and often was a result of questions posed by them. His teaching was personalized and he also gained their involvement. He started where the learners were at.

8. Jesus practiced "learning by doing" as seen in most of his teaching and learning experiences. There were always opportunity to respond by doing, e.g., go, sin no more, go and do likewise, go and teach, stretch out your hand, etc.

The Christian teacher participates in actions intended to help students learn about the revelation of God and his requirements for humanity.

Tom and Joani Shultz gave the following necessary suggestions for success in teaching:

1. Stress learning over teaching
2. Zero in on what is most important
3. Emphasize understanding
4. Promote thinking
5. Use active learning
6. Use interactive learning
7. Stick to your goal

3.8 Recommendations to Rekindle the Flame of Christian Education

This study has explored the history and biblical principles of education from its initial stage to the present time. Significant changes were noted, resulting in a definite decline from the fundamental principles of former Christian educators but most of all from the original instructions given by God in Deut 6. We have seen how these God given instructions were successfully carried out by Moses, Jesus and many others. However, this paper highlighted several factors, events, individuals as well as new philosophies that have influenced the biblical principles of education which resulted in what is known as secular education.

It is highly unlikely that Christian educators employed by secular institutions would have any moral or spiritual influence on the curriculum. The reason being, the curriculum is designed according to the philosophy of the school. Should there be any attempts to modify the prescribed program of study according to one's own religious convictions the Christian educator would no doubt be faced with serious challenges and oppositions. The following are some things that Christian educators can do in their effort to rekindle the flame of Christian education:

1. Be ready to teach biblical principles anytime, anywhere and to anyone as was instructed in Deut chapter 6.

2. Be a "School Planter", i.e. establish Christian schools whenever and wherever possible, offering Christian education at an affordable cost. Start with your home church, if they do not already have a Christian school.

3. Become a distributor of free Christian based Bible courses. Courses are available from "Source of Light" and other ministries.

4. Support and promote Christian education.

5. Have your church designate one week of activities per year as "Christian Education Week" and commence the week's activities with a special church service highlighting Christian education.

6. Become a qualified Christian school teacher or a Sunday school teacher and give it your best shot.

7. Raise funds to sponsor students in Christian schools or theological seminaries.

8. Maintain relevance in Christian education by pursuing regular training courses, attend seminars, retreats, or attend a Bible study and or study of related subjects.

The following recommendation can be utilized to initiate a Christian Education Awareness Week.

Christian Education Awareness

The objective is to set aside one entire week per year as Christian Education Awareness Week. During this time educators would meet to evaluate reform and/or introduce new strategies, developments or approaches to Christian education. The week can include a series of promotional events such as an open house at the Christian school facility where parents can get familiar with the work of the school. Commence Christian education week with a church service when emphasis would be placed on the importance of Christian education. The service can include activities from the various sections of the education department of the church and school. An example of a program of events follows:

1. Showcase of talents – music, drama, dance, songs, solo items including poetry, etc.

2. Obtain promotional items for distribution to individuals.

3. Special offering to be collected for ongoing development and expansion of Christian education.

4. The life and work of one significant contributor to Christian education is to be featured throughout the week as the "Torch Bearer". This person has to be one who has greatly contributed to the history of Christian education, for example, Martin Luther.

5. Pass out brochures to inform people of the various Christian education programs available.

6. This time should also be used, attract and enroll new students.

7. "The Torchbearer of the Year Award" - Recognize one local Christian educator for this award, someone who has significantly contributed to Christian education in the local schools.

3.9 Conclusion

Gone are the days of cultivating Christian character or what is godly, right or true in our public Schools. The battle is raging for the minds of the children of this generation. But there is hope and we, as Christian educators must rise to the challenge and stand tall against the evil schemes of the enemy to eradicate God and the Bible from schools and society. We must rise up and make a difference through the promotion and support of Christian Education. We must restore the old principles, and return to the ancient paths that were hewed for us.

In the following text, Moses highlights the educational mandate of Deut. 6 given to him by God. This passage gives us a wonderful insight about the student, the curriculum, the setting and the goals of the teacher of biblical education. This mandate also stressed the further commands of God to preserve and pass the teachings down from generation to generation:

> *"These are the commands, decrees and laws the Lord your God directed me to teach you to observe in the land that you are crossing the Jordan to possess, so that you, your children and their children after them may fear the Lord your God as long as you live by keeping all his decrees and commands that I give you, and so that you may enjoy long life.*
>
> *Hear, O Israel; The Lord our God, the Lord is one, Love the Lord your God with all your heart and with all your soul and with all your strength. These commandments that I give you today are to be upon your hearts. Impress them on your children. Talk about them when you sit at home and when you walk along the road, when you lie down and when you get up. Tie them as symbols on your hands and bind then on your foreheads.*

> *Write them on the door frames of your houses and on your gates. (Deut. 6:1-2; 4-9)*

Deut 30:11-20 also stresses the importance of obedience to this commandment outlining the issues at stake if we neglect these educational principles. Failure to obey these commands will result in curses and warnings as follows:

> *See, I set before you today life and prosperity, death and destruction; For I command you today to love the Lord your God, to walk in his ways, and to keep his commands, decrees and laws; than you will live and increase, and the Lord your God will bless you in the land you are entering to possess.*
>
> *But if your heart turns away and you are not obedient, and if you are drawn away to bow down to other gods and worship them, I declare to you this day that you will certainly be destroyed. You will not live long in the land you are crossing the Jordan to enter and possess.*
>
> *This day I call heaven and earth as witnesses against you that I have set before you life and death, blessings and curses. Now choose life, so that you and your children may live and that you may love the Lord your God, listen to his voice, and hold fast to him, For the Lord is your life and he will give you many years in the land he swore to give to your fathers, Abraham, Isaac and Jacob.*

The above verses may be considered God's prescribed method for effective education. Accordingly, there are consequences for all those who refuse to comply with these standards. Therefore it is imperative that those of the household of faith *"go and teach all nations"*. We are challenged, to utilize every available means and resources for the advancement of Christian education.

Finally, if we are to be successful in impacting this present generation by transforming lives for the kingdom of God, the time to re-evaluate and reform our current educational goals and strategies is now. We MUST make a concerted effort to rekindle the flame of Christian education.

Bibliography

Byrne, H.W., Christian Education in the Local Church, Zondervan Publishing House, Grand Rapids, Mi: 1998

Clarke, Catherine K., Ph.D.. A Revolution in Education is Needed, www/onoi.org/rms/wcc.html

Darville, P. A & W. R. Stirling,.The Expanding Years, Schoefield & Simms Ltd. London, 1973

Galindo, Israel The craft of Christian teaching, Judson Press, Valley Forge, Pa. 1998

Gangel, Kenneth O. & Warren S. Benson, Christian Ed. Its History & Philosophy, Moody Press, Chicago, 1983

Gregory, John Milton, The Seven Laws of Teaching, Baker Book House, Grand Rapids, Mich, 1992

Greng, Stanley J., Gurepzki & Wordling, Cherith S. in Pocket dictionary of Theological Terms 2nd ed., s.v.

Horne, Herman, Jesus the Teacher, Kregel Publication, Grand Rapids, Mi.: 1998

Jeffrey, Grant R. Prince of Darkness, Bantam Books, New York NY, 1995

Moore, Raymond S., Adventist Education at the Crossroads, Pacific Press Publishing Assn, Mountain View, Ca. 1976

New Standard Encyclopedia, 1980

Pazmiño, Robert W. Fundamental Issues in Christian Education, Baker Books, Grand Rapids, Mi. 1997

Pazmiño, Robert W., Principles & Practices of Christian Education, Baker Book House, Grand Rapids, Mich. 1992

Rhone, D. D. Min., West Indies Union Visitor, 1st Quarter, 2002

Schmidt, Alvin J. Under the influence, Zondervan Publishing House, Grand Rapids, MI 2001

Shepherd, Gene D. & Ragan, Modern Elementary Curriculum, Harcourt Brace Jovanovich College Publishers, Fort Worth, TX, 1991

Shultz, Tom & Joani, Why Nobody Learns Much Of Anything In Church, Group, Loveland Colorado, 1993

Sikkama, K., The rebirth of learning and the reformation, Internet web page

Smith, Jim L., One Nation Under God or Man?, Smith Publications, Lawrenceburg Tn: 1989

Tyler, Dr. Glenn E. Be Successful in Your Ministry II, Tyler Crusades, Inc., Plymouth, FL

White, Ellen G, Education, Pacific Press Publishing Association, Boise, Idaho: 1952

About the Author

Mrs. D. (Judy) Williams is the founder of the Maranatha Theological Institute. The mission of the Institute is to "Stomp out Biblical Illiteracy" by facilitating theological training courses. She serves as Supervisor and Lecturer for the International Seminary (Plymouth, Florida) off campus Satellite Class in the Cayman Islands.

Mrs. Williams is a 1974 Graduate of the Cayman Islands High School. She pursued further education at the Cayman Islands Community College, South West London College (UK) and International Seminary. She holds theological Diplomas from International Seminary, and a degree in Religious Education (B.R.Ed.) from Christian Bible College of Rocky Mount Inc. NC.

She is married to Anthony Williams and has three sons, Lehron, Lorin & Joshua.

Endnotes

[1] Ellen G. White, Education, p 13

[2] Robert W. Pazmiño, Foundational Issues in Christian Education, p 86-87

[3] Ibid, p 87

[4] Ibid, p 88

[5] Dr. Glenn E. Tyler, I.S. Lecture 118 – Christian Education Pt 1, p 4

[6] Robert W. Pazmiño, Foundational Issues in Christian Education p135

[7] Herman Horne, Jesus the Teacher, p 11 - 12

[8] Alvin J. Schmidt, Under the influence, p 171

[9] Ibid, p 172

[10] Ibid, p 173

[11] Israel Galindo, The craft of Christian teaching, p 62

[12] Ibid, pg 62

[13] Robert W. Pazmiño, Foundational I Issues in Christian Education, p 132

[14] Dr. Glenn E. Tyler, Be Successful in Your Ministry II, Lecture 86 p 2

[15] Robert W. Pazmiño, Foundational Issues in Christian Education, p 145

[16] K Sikkama, The rebirth of Learning and the Reformation, Internet web page

[17] Ibid, Internet web page

[18] Gangel & Benson, Christian Ed. Its History & Philosophy, p 141

[19] Ibid, p 128

[20] Ibid, p 128

[21] Alvin J. Schmidt, Under the influence pg 172)

[22] Ibid, p 199

[23] Gangel & Benson, Christian Ed. Its History & Philosophy, p 177

[24] Robert W. Pazmiño, Foundational Issues in Christian Education, p 147

[25] New Standard Encyclopedia, s.v.

[26] Pocket dictionary of Theological Terms, s.v.

[27] Gangel & Benson, Christian Ed. Its History & Philosophy, p154

[28] Ibid, p 159

[29] Ibid, p 175

[30] Ibid, p 173

[31] P. A. Darville, The Expanding Years, p 198

[32] Jim L. Smith, One Nation Under God or Man?, p 9

[33] Ibid, p 10

[34] Ibid, p 16

[35] Ibid, p 35

[36] Ibid, p 15

[37] Ibid, p 38

[38] Ibid, p 38

[39] Dr. Glenn E. Tyler, Be Successful in Your Ministry II – Lecture # 100, p 1

[40] Gangel & Benson, Christian Ed. Its History & Philosophy, p 303

[41] Dr. Glenn E. Tyler, Be Successful in Your Ministry II – Lecture # 120

[42] Lucis (Lucifer) Trust, Alice Bailey & Works, etc. Webpage www/conspiracyarchive/com/new age/lucis_trust.

[43] Ibid, p 2

[44] http//www.unoi.org/rms/wcc.htm, A Revolution in Education is Needed, p 2

[45] Ibid, p 2

[46] Grant R. Jeffrey, Prince of Darkness, p 87

[47] Jim L. Smith, One Nation Under God or Man?, p 18

[48] D. Rhone D. Min., West Indies Union Visitor, p 23

[49] H.W. Byrne, Christian Education in the Local Church, 225

[50] Robert W. Pazmiño, Foundational Issues in Christian Education, p 224

[51] Ibid, p 224

[52] Robert W. Pazmiňo, Foundational Issues in Christian Education, p 225

[53] Gene D. Shepherd & Williams B. Ragan, Modern Elementary Curriculum, 215-217

[54] Hilda Tabam Curriculum Development: Theory & practice, p 12

[55] H.W. Byrne, Christian Education in the Local Church, 227-228

[56] Ibid, p 249-250

[57] Raymond S. Moore, Adventist Education at the Crossroads, p 94

[58] John Milton Gregory, The Seven Laws of Teaching

Printed in the United Kingdom
by Lightning Source UK Ltd.
101684UKS00002B/196-294